CHARITABLE GIVING GUIDE FOR SHORT-TERM MISSION TRIPS

DAN BUSBY • MICHAEL MARTIN • JOHN VAN DRUNEN

This publication is designed to provide accurate and authoritative information regarding the subject matter covered. The text has been significantly excerpted from *The Guide to Charitable Giving for Churches and Ministries.* It is distributed with the understanding that neither the publisher nor the authors are engaged in rendering legal, accounting, or other professional services. If legal advice or other expert assistance is required, the services of a competent professional person should be sought.

Every effort has been made to make the materials in this text current as of the date of publication. Federal tax law, however, is subject to change. Congress can modify the law as it has on numerous occasions over the years. Also, court decisions and IRS rulings can significantly affect the application of federal tax laws. Such changes may affect the accuracy of this publication.

Revised Edition, 2016

ISBN: 978-1-936233-14-4

The Authors

Dan Busby is president of ECFA, an organization that accredits Christ-centered churches and ministries in the areas of governance, financial management, and stewardship/fundraising. ECFA's seal enhances the trust of givers, which increases generosity, and provides greater resources to help fulfill the Great Commission. Founded in 1979, ECFA now accredits 2,000 churches and ministries across the United States. Together, these organizations have annual revenue of $25 billion.

Dan frequently speaks nationally on church and ministry issues. He has authored or co-authored six titles with more than 50 total volumes. His latest book is *TRUST: The Firm Foundation for Kingdom Fruitfulness.* He has been recognized for six consecutive years on the *NonProfit Times'* Power & Influence Top 50 list and honored in the Hall of Fame of the National Association of Church Business Administration.

Dan served as a member of the Commission on Accountability and Policy for Religious Organizations, a national legislative advisory commission convened to address legislative proposals to the U.S. Congress for the nonprofit sector.

Michael Martin serves as ECFA's vice president and legal counsel. He graduated with a bachelor of arts in government, *summa cum laude*, from Oral Roberts University and a juris doctor from Regent University School of Law, where he was editor-in-chief of the *Regent University Law Review.*

Michael is passionate about helping churches and ministries with legal and tax-related issues and compliance with ECFA standards. In addition to authoring and reviewing articles and other resources featured in ECFA publications, he assists with member compliance and leads ECFA's church initiative.

Beginning with the 2013 edition, Michael co-authored the *Zondervan Minister's Tax & Financial Guide* and the *Zondervan Church and Nonprofit Tax & Financial Guide* with Dan Busby and John Van Drunen.

John Van Drunen is executive vice president and general counsel of ECFA, with a bachelor of arts in accounting, *magna cum laude*, from Anderson University and a juris doctor from Regent University School of Law.

John oversees the compliance process for ECFA including renewals, applications, compliance concerns, and site visits, in addition to serving as in-house general counsel. John was extensively involved in the work of the Commission on Accountability and Policy for Religious Organizations and the Religious Organizations Accounting Committee.

Beginning with the 2010 edition, John co-authored the *Zondervan Minister's Tax & Financial Guide* and the *Zondervan Church and Nonprofit Tax & Financial Guide* with Dan Busby and Michael Martin.

Introduction

Many charities, including churches and parachurch organizations, sponsor individuals that serve on domestic and international short-term mission trips.

The proper handling of funds raised and expended for short-term mission trips often presents challenging tax, finance, and legal issues for trip participants and sending organizations alike. The administration of these trips is an opportunity for churches and other charities to model excellence, integrity, and compliance with the law.

We trust this simple, how-to guide by ECFA—including numerous examples and sample illustrations—will help you and your organization as you serve the Kingdom through missions!

Contributions for Short-Term Mission Trips

Executive Summary

- Participants in short-term mission trips are often responsible to raise part or all of the expenses relating to the trip.
- To qualify for a charitable contribution deduction, the giver's intent must be to benefit the ministry rather than an individual.
- The ministry sponsoring the trip is responsible to demonstrate discretion and control over gifts given for short-term mission trips.
- If a ministry sponsors a mission trip which is not for pleasure or personal gain, gifts for the trip are generally tax-deductible, even if given by a trip participant.
- If intended trip participants choose not go on a mission trip, the sponsoring ministry should follow a policy of not refunding gifts related to the trip. Refunding gifts for short-term mission trips may jeopardize the tax-deductibility of all amounts paid for the ministry's mission trips.

Contributions for Short-Term Mission Trips

Ministries may fund short-term mission trips in a variety of ways. First, a *sponsoring organization* could pay part or all of a trip's expenses from the ministry's general budget. Second, *trip participants* could cover a trip's costs directly without any financial involvement of the sponsoring ministry. The most common approach, however, is for supporters (trip participants or other givers) to fund a short-term trip through *charitable gifts to the sponsoring ministry.* These gifts may be restricted by givers for a particular trip or project conducted by the sponsoring ministry. Givers may also indicate a *preference* to support the work of an individual trip participant, but givers who *restrict* gifts for trip participants jeopardize the tax-deductibility of their charitable contributions.

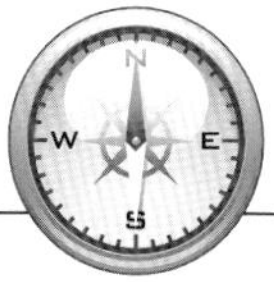

Remember

Single contributions of $250 or more for short-term mission trips require a written acknowledgment.

If a giver makes a single contribution of $250 or more in paying short-term mission trip expenses, the giver must have—and the ministry should provide—a written contemporaneous acknowledgment (see example on page 23).

- **Funding from the sponsoring ministry's general budget.**

  Expenses relating to short-term mission trips may be funded in full by the sponsoring ministry. This use of funds from the sponsoring ministry's general budget is appropriate if short-term mission trips are consistent with its tax-exempt purposes.

- **Funds directly expended by the trip participant with no financial involvement of the sponsoring ministry.**

A participant in a short-term mission trip may partially or totally fund trip expenses by making direct payments for airfare, lodging, meals, and other expenses. If a trip is sponsored by a ministry, the trip is consistent with the tax-exempt purposes of the ministry, and there is no significant element of personal pleasure, recreation or vacation,[1] expenses related to the trip are generally deductible as charitable contributions on the taxpayer's Schedule A, Itemized Deductions. The deduction will not be denied simply because the taxpayer enjoys providing services to the ministry.[2] Personal expenses relating to "side-trips" or vacation days unrelated to the mission trip included in the trip are generally not deductible.

- **Funding based on gifts for the trip but with no preference in relation to any trip participant.**

Givers may make gifts restricted for a short-term mission trip. Gifts for the trip could be solicited by the ministry, or the giver might make an unsolicited gift. These gifts generally qualify as charitable contributions, and it is appropriate for the sponsoring ministry to provide a charitable gift acknowledgment.

If a ministry accepts gifts that are giver-restricted for a short-term mission trip, the ministry is obligated to spend the funds for the intended purpose.

It is true that a giver could change the gift restriction by redirecting the gift for another specified purpose or unrestrict the gift. This scenario presumes the donated funds have not already been expended or obligated for the mission trip.

Additionally, a ministry could establish, and disclose with gift solicitation information, a board policy regarding the possible redirection of giver-restricted gifts if a mission trip event is canceled or oversubscribed (more funds are received than needed).

- **Funding based on gifts preferenced for particular trip participants.**

Generally, mission trip participants are responsible for soliciting gifts to cover part or all of the expenses necessary for the particular trip (see pages 21–22 for a sample letter from a potential short-term mission trip participant to a potential giver).

When mission trip participants raise part or all of the funds required for a trip, the sponsoring ministry generally accounts for the amounts preferenced for particular participants. This process allows the ministry to monitor whether sufficient funds have been raised to cover the expenses for each individual's trip.

There is generally no basis for refunding gifts if the individual for which gifts have been preferenced does not go on the trip. Refunding gifts demonstrates that the sponsoring ministry does not have adequate discretion and control over the gifts and may raise a question of the tax-deductibility of the gifts.

Remember

Gifts preferenced for particular trip participants should generally not be refunded to donors if the preferenced individual does not go on the trip.

When a worker or a volunteer (a short-term mission trip participant typically qualifies as a "volunteer") raises some of his or her own support, the IRS has suggested the following two tests to determine whether a tax-deductible contribution was made to or for the use of a ministry, or whether the gift was a nondeductible, pass-through gift to a particular individual who ultimately benefited from the contribution.[3]

1. **The intended benefit test.** The purpose of this test is to determine whether the contributor's intent in making the donation was to benefit the ministry or the individual.

   The IRS has formally indicated that ministries should avoid the use of conflicting language in their solicitations for contributions and conflicts in understandings between the parties. This is to demonstrate that

   a. The ministry has exercised the necessary control over contributions;

   b. The giver has reason to know that the ministry will have the necessary discretion and control over contributions; and

   c. The giver intends for the ministry to be the actual recipient of the contributions.

   The authors recommend the following statement be used in solicitations for contributions:

   Contributions are solicited with the understanding that [insert name of sponsoring ministry] has complete discretion and control over the use of all donated funds.

2. **The discretion and control test.** The IRS uses the phrase "discretion and control" to indicate a ministry's obligation regarding charitable gifts. The IRS has stated that ministries receiving funds for the support of mission endeavors can demonstrate discretion and control with the following factors:

   a. Reimbursement of legitimate ministry expenses are approved by the ministry, consistent with the governing body's guidelines. Reimbursement should be set by considerations other than the amount of money collected by the individuals who raise funds.

   b. Potential trip members are screened according to qualifications established by the ministry.

   c. Trip members are given meaningful training, development, and supervision.

   d. The ministry assigns trip members to programs and project locations based upon its assessment of each individual's skills and training, and the specific needs of the ministry.

Remember

Apply both the intended benefit test and the discretion and control test when soliciting and administering funds related to short-term mission trips.

   e. Giver acknowledgments communicate the ministry's full discretion and control over its programs and funds.

   f. Since the ministry should not accept contributions restricted to or for a particular person, communication by potential trip participants to potential givers should not indicate otherwise. A giver may indicate a preference that the ministry use a gift to support a certain individual's trip, and the ministry may track the dollars based on that preference. However, the ministry and the potential trip participant should refrain from any inference that the contributions will be paid as expenses to or for a particular worker.[4]

Even if the intended benefit and discretion and control tests are met, there may be charitable tax-deductibility issues based on age of trip participants (see Example 2 on page 8), ministry authorization, and the pursuit of pleasure or personal gain. Two potentially tax-deductible scenarios follow.

Example 1: **Trip participants are adults.** These two examples illustrate different funding patterns when trip participants are adults:

a. **Participants contribute to the ministry to cover part or all of the trip expenses.** The payments by the participants to the ministry are deductible as charitable contributions if the trip involves no significant element of personal pleasure, recreation, or vacation. These trip contributions may be acknowledged by the ministry as charitable contributions.

b. **All trip expenses are paid by the ministry, and non-participants make contributions to cover trip expenses.** If the ministry has preauthorized the mission trip, the trip furthers the exempt purposes of the ministry, and if the trip involves no significant element of personal pleasure, recreation, or vacation, then gifts to cover the trip expenses are generally tax-deductible, even if the givers indicate a preference that gifts be applied to the trip expenses of a particular participant.

Example 2: **Trip participants are minors.** If a trip participant is a minor, the minor must actually provide services to carry out the tax-exempt purposes of the trip. The age of the minor and the minor's development may be important factors in determining the minor's capability of providing services to the ministry.

If parents, relatives, and/or friends contribute to the ministry with a preference for a child's trip expenses and the ministry pays the trip expenses, these contributions are generally tax-deductible, assuming the minor significantly contributes to the trip purposes.

Remember

Earmarked gifts should generally not be accepted by an organization sponsoring a mission trip.

- **Funding based on gifts *restricted* for a particular trip participant.**

A giver may express a *preference* for a particular trip recipient, but if a giver expresses a *restriction* for a certain trip recipient, the gift is generally an earmarked gift. Therefore, the gift may not qualify for a charitable deduction and should generally not be accepted (or not acknowledged as a charitable gift if accepted).

Sponsors of short-term mission trips generally should not accept gifts earmarked for individuals because the gifts are not consistent with the ministry's tax-exempt purposes. An earmarked gift is a transfer that is intended to benefit an individual, not the ministry ("for Joe Smith's trip costs"). It is a transfer over which the ministry does not have sufficient discretion and control.

- **Accounting for short-term mission trips.**

Gifts that qualify for the issuance of charitable gift acknowledgments by a ministry should be recorded as charitable gift revenue by the sponsoring ministry. If earmarked gifts are accepted by the sponsoring ministry, the amounts should generally be treated as agency funds and reflected as a liability on the ministry's statement of financial position.

Some sponsoring ministries initially record gifts preferenced for particular trip participants as a liability until the trip is complete and then reclassify the transaction as a charitable gift. This is done in an effort to justify any refunds for gifts preferenced for potential trip participants who did not go on the trip. This practice is inconsistent with the need to exercise discretion and control over the gifts and could jeopardize the tax deductibility of the gifts; therefore, the practice is not recommended.

Gifts for short-term mission trips will generally qualify for recording as donor-restricted revenue. This is because a short-term mission trip usually represents a purpose that is more specific than the broad limits imposed by the ministry's purpose and nature.

Review

1. **Are gifts to support short-term mission trips deductible as charitable gifts?** Generally, yes, but it depends on the facts and circumstances. To be tax-deductible, gifts preferenced to support a trip participant must be subject to the discretion and control of the sponsoring ministry, the trip must be for legitimate mission purposes, and the trip participants must fulfill those purposes.

2. **Is it appropriate for a ministry to sponsor and fund a short-term mission trip with funds in the ministry's general budget or with funds raised for a short-term mission trip project (givers did not indicate a preference to support any particular participant)?** Yes, if the purposes of the trip are consistent with the tax-exempt purposes of the ministry and there is no significant element of personal pleasure, recreation, or vacation with respect to the participants.

3. **Can short-term mission trip participants pay part or all of the trip expenses, with no financial involvement of the sponsoring ministry?** Yes, if the trip is sponsored or approved by the ministry,

the trip is consistent with the tax-exempt purposes of the ministry, and there is no significant element of personal pleasure, recreation, or vacation. If the trip meets these thresholds, the ministry may provide a written charitable contribution acknowledgment to the trip participant for out-of-pocket expenses.

4. **Is it appropriate for givers to indicate a preference or express a desire that a gift be used to fund the trip of a particular participant, even if the giver is the trip participant or a relative?** If only a preference is made for the gift to be used to fund the expenses of a particular participant, preferenced gifts are generally deductible if the trip is sponsored or approved by the ministry, the trip is consistent with the tax-exempt purposes of the ministry, and there is no significant element of personal pleasure, recreation, or vacation.

5. **Are funds given to a ministry deductible when the gifts are preferenced for particular trip participants and the participants are minors?** It depends. The minor must actually provide services to carry out the tax-exempt purposes of the trip. The age of the minor and the minor's development may be important factors in determining the minor's capability of providing services to the ministry.

6. **Should gifts ever be refunded to givers when a potential short-term mission trip participant does not go on the trip and gifts have been preferenced for that individual?** Generally, no. Sponsoring ministries should have a policy prohibiting refunds of gifts relating to short-term mission trips. Refunding a mission trip gift demonstrates a lack of discretion and control by the sponsoring ministry over gifts, thereby placing the tax-deductibility of the gifts at risk.

Exhibits

Churches and charitable organizations have permission to use, duplicate, and customize these sample policies in carrying out their mission programs. These policies are distributed with the understanding neither the publisher nor the authors are engaged in rendering legal, accounting, or other professional services. If legal advice or other expert assistance is required, the services of a competent professional person should be sought.

Sample Short-Term Mission Trip and Mission Field Assessment Visit Policy

ABC Ministry occasionally sponsors short-term mission trips. While these trips may provide essential ministry services and encouragement on the field, the visits are primarily intended to introduce trip participants to missions.

Additionally, it is often desirable for ministry staff and/or volunteers to visit a supported missionary (national or expatriate) in the field, assess a potential field of service for potential future missionary support, or assess a potential field of service for a future short-term mission trip. Visits to missionaries currently supported by the ministry are to (1) demonstrate the ministry's commitment to their ministry, (2) provide face-to-face encouragement, and (3) assess the effectiveness of the ministry.

The ministry desires that God will be honored in every aspect of these trips. Therefore, this policy has been developed and adopted by the ministry's Governing Board to provide general guidance for these trips.

Trip approval. All short-term mission trips and field assessment visits are recommended by the ministry's executive leadership to be considered under these policies. (*Note:* The trip approval process will vary based on the governance structure of a particular ministry.)

Approval, training, supervision and assignment of trip participants. Potential non-staff trip members will be screened according to qualifications established by the ministry and trip participants are given meaningful training and adequately supervised.

Sample Short-Term Mission Trip and Mission Field Assessment Visit Policy *(continued)*

Non-staff trip participants are assigned to programs and project locations based on the ministry's assessment of each individual's skills and training.

Funding trips. Based on the funding method approved by the ministry for a particular trip, the following funding approaches may be used:

A. Trip expenses may be fully or partially funded by the ministry. Funds from the missions or other budget line items may be identified for this purpose.

B. Trip expenses may be fully or partially funded through resources raised by the trip participants. Funding may be raised to cover direct and indirect trip costs, based on the approval of the funding plan by the ministry. While the ministry will accept gifts preferenced for the trip of a particular participant, the ministry will not accept gifts restricted or designated for a particular trip participant. (Reason: Gifts restricted or designated for a particular trip participant do not qualify to receive a charitable gift acknowledgment and such gifts are not consistent with the tax-exempt status of the ministry.)

If trip expenses are fully or partially funded by resources raised by the trip participants, all communication to givers—sample text for letters, websites and blog posting, and talking points for the verbal communication about the trip—will be approved by the ministry.

If resources are raised beyond the goal for a particular trip participant, the excess may be used to provide resources for a trip participant who is under-funded.

Sample Short-Term Mission Trip and Mission Field Assessment Visit Policy *(continued)*

If the resources raised by a potential trip participant are fewer than the financial goal established by the ministry, the ministry will determine whether to assign funds sufficient to allow the individual to participate in the trip. The additional funds could come from the ministry's mission or general funds, or the additional funds could come from resources raised beyond the goal of other trip participants.

Issuing charitable gift acknowledgments. At the discretion of the ministry, charitable gift acknowledgments will be prepared by the church and provided for all gifts that conform with this policy, including gifts from family members and trip participants. However, gifts will not be acknowledged if the trip participant is unable to, or for any reason does not plan to, significantly perform services to carry out the purposes of the trip (for example, a child of age three).

The ministry will determine the appropriateness of issuing charitable gift acknowledgments when trip participants pay their own expenses for a ministry-sponsored trip. No charitable gift acknowledgments will be issued for short-term mission trips that have not been approved by the ministry.

Charitable gift acknowledgments issued by the ministry will include the following wording:

- An indication the ministry has discretion and control over the gifts
- A statement indicating "no goods or services were provided in exchange for the gifts," if this is true.

Sample Short-Term Mission Trip and Mission Field Assessment Visit Policy *(continued)*

In determining whether a gift is preferenced or restricted for a potential trip participant, the ministry will use the following principles for guidance:

- A preferenced gift merely comes with a preference or a desire that the gift be used to support the trip expenses of a particular trip participant.

  Preferenced gifts generally may be accepted with a gift acknowledgment provided.

- An earmarked gift is a transfer that is intended to benefit an individual, not the ministry. It is a transfer over which the ministry does not have sufficient discretion and control. For example, if accepted, the ministry would not have the freedom to use the funds for a trip participant who fell short of the financial goal for the trip.

  Earmarked gifts generally should not be accepted; therefore, a gift acknowledgment is a moot issue.

Refunding of gifts related to trips. Gifts preferenced for particular gift recipients will not be refunded to givers except in unusual circumstances, such as the cancellation of a trip. Funds preferenced for the trip of a particular participant could be carried forward for a future trip as the discretion of the ministry.

Discretion and control over gifts. All gifts given to support trips are the property of the ministry and will be expended under the discretion and control of the ministry.

Accounting records. The ministry will separately record revenue and expense related to each short-term mission trip.

Sample Short-Term Mission Trip and Mission Field Assessment Visit Policy *(continued)*

Determining accountable expenses related to trips. Expenses will be reimbursed under the ministry's accountable expense reimbursement plan. Allowable volunteer expenses include transportation expenses and reasonable expenses for meals and lodging necessarily incurred while away from home. Expenses will not be reimbursed for individuals who only have nominal duties relating to the performance of services for the ministry or who for significant portions of the trip are not required to render services.

While "a significant element of personal pleasure" is not defined by the tax code or regulations, the current edition of IRS publication 526 provides the following guidance:

> Generally, you can claim a charitable contribution deduction for travel expenses necessarily incurred while you are away from home performing services for a charitable organization only if there is no significant element of personal pleasure, recreation, or vacation in the travel. This applies whether you pay for the expenses directly or indirectly. You are paying the expenses indirectly if you make a payment to the charitable organization and the organization pays for your travel expenses.
>
> The deduction for travel expenses will not be denied simply because you enjoy providing services to the charitable organization. Even if you enjoy the trip, you can take a charitable contribution deduction for your travel expenses if you are on duty in a genuine and substantial sense throughout the trip. However, if you have

Sample Short-Term Mission Trip and Mission Field Assessment Visit Policy *(continued)*

only nominal duties, or if for significant parts of the trip you do not have any duties, you cannot deduct your travel expenses.

To prove the extent and duration of services, each trip participant will keep an hour-by-hour itinerary of the entire trip. The itinerary should separate those times when the trip participant is on duty for the ministry from those times when the participant is free to choose his or her own activities.

Ministry staff participation in trips. Ministry staff are encouraged to participate in mission trips by providing them with one week of paid time for one trip per year subject to the approval of the staff member's supervisor. (Note: Your ministry may determine it is appropriate for staff to have more paid time for trips; for example, two weeks of paid time for up to two trips per year.)

Staff members are responsible to raise the same financial support as other trip participants. (*Note:* Your ministry may determine it is appropriate for a staff member who is leading a team to raise support for the team as a whole, whereby the funding for the leader is paid from the overall trip budget.)

If a staff participant is a non-exempt employee for purposes of the Fair Labor Standards Act, and the mission trip responsibilities are not clearly outside the scope of their position description, the ministry will define the hours on- and off-duty during the trip to clearly determine any overtime hours. (*Note:* Your ministry may determine that staff members participating outside the scope of their position description must use leave time instead of receiving their regular pay.)

Sample Short-Term Mission Trip Support-Raising Letter

This short-term mission trip support-raising letter demonstrates elements which follow IRS guidance. The notes in the letter relate to accounting for the gift and qualifying it for a tax deduction.

1232 Main Street
Yakima, WA 98904
509/248-6739

Date

Dear Mr. and Mrs. Giver,

> This paragraph confirms it is a church-sponsored mission trip.

This summer, I have an exciting opportunity to serve the Lord on a mission trip sponsored by our church (Yakima Fellowship) to East Africa. Fifteen members of my church youth group plan to participate in a 10-day trip. We will fly into Nairobi, Kenya, on July 21.

> This paragraph confirms that ministry will be performed on the trip.

Our ministry during this trip is in Nairobi at an orphanage where most of the children have AIDS. Our team will lead a Vacation Bible School, distribute clothes we will take with us, and be available to work with and support the children in the orphanage. Sponsors from our church will accompany our team and provide ministry oversight.

One of the ways you can help me is to pray for the trip, the ministry we will perform, and for me personally. Only with a prayer support will I be able to bless the children in the orphanage.

> This paragraph confirms that gifts are preferenced for Jodi's trip expenses. (For accounting purposes, gifts are temporarily restricted for the mission trip.)

Yes, there are financial needs. The cost of the trip is $2,100, which each team member is responsible to raise in gifts for our church. Please pray with me that the funds to cover my trip expenses will be provided.

Gifts to the church, with an expression of a preference for my trip expenses, are tax deductible to the extent allowed by law.

> This paragraph confirms the church will exercise discretion and control over the funds. Implied is "There are no refunds to givers if I don't go."

If you will commit to pray, please check the appropriate box on the enclosed card. If you are able to make a gift to the church to assist with my expenses, please check the appropriate box on the card, indicating your interest in helping fund my portion of the trip expenses, and make your check payable to the sponsoring church, Yakima Fellowship. If I am unable to participate in the trip, your gifts will be used to support the short-term mission program of the church.

May God bless you richly as you consider your involvement in this mission trip!

Sincerely,
Jodi Hunter

Sample Short-Term Mission Trip Response Form

(Trip Expenses Paid by the Ministry)

We want to support the missions outreach of Yakima Fellowship and are sending our gift of $____________.

Our preference is that this gift be used to support the short-term mission trip of Jodi Hunter. We understand that the use of the gift is subject to the discretion and control of Yakima Fellowship.

Giver(s):
Bill and Karen Smith
2315 Main
Wenatchee, WA 98801

> These paragraphs make it clear that the giver's intent is to benefit the ministry. Their financial support of Jodi Hunter is simply a desire.

Sample Short-Term Mission Trip Gift Acknowledgment

(Trip Expenses Paid by the Ministry)

Official Acknowledgment • Please keep this acknowledgment for your tax records

	Preferenced for the mission trip of:	Total Amount	Gift Amount	Other Amount
Acknowledgment #2675 Gift Date: 01/02/XX Acknowledgment Date: 01/15/XX Bill and Karen Smith 2315 Main Wenatchee, WA 98801	Jodi Hunter	$100	$100	0

Thank you for your contribution which is tax-deductible to the extent allowed by law. While every effort will be made to apply your gift according to an indicated preference, if any, **Yakima Fellowship** has complete discretion and control over the use of the donated funds. We thank God for you and appreciate your support.

Other than reflected on this acknowledgment, no goods or services, in part or in whole, were provided in exchange for this gift.

Yakima Fellowship
PO Box 4256
Yakima, WA 98904
509/248-5555

ECFA MEMBER

Sample Short-Term Mission Trip Gift Check

(Trip Expenses Paid by the Ministry)

Bill and Karen Smith
2315 Main
Wenatchee, WA 98801

DATE: *December 31, 20XX*

PAY TO THE ORDER OF: *Yakima Fellowship* $ *200.00*

Two Hundred and no/100 ---------------------------------- DOLLARS

FOR *Missions Work*

Bill Smith

Note: If a giver wishes to identify the preferenced participant on the check, to avoid communicating the gift is earmarked for a particular participant. It is more advisable for the giver to check an appropriately-worded box on the response form to indicate a preference to support the ministry of a particular trip participant.

Sample Short-Term Mission Trip Gift Acknowledgment

(Trip Expenses Paid by the Participant)

Official Acknowledgment • Please keep this acknowledgment for your tax records

Acknowledgment #4575 Gift Date: 01/02/XX Acknowledgment Date: 01/15/XX Bill and Karen Smith 2315 Main Wenatchee, WA 98801	**Description of Services Provided**	**Built church building in Nairobi, Kenya, on July 21-28, 20XX**

Thank you for your contribution which are tax-deductible to the extent allowed by law. While every effort will be made to apply your gift according to an indicated preference, if any, **Yakima Fellowship** has complete discretion and control over the use of the donated funds. We thank God for you and appreciate your support.

Yakima Fellowship
PO Box 4256
Yakima, WA 98904
509/248-5555

Other than reflected on this acknowledgment, no goods or services, in part or in whole, were provided in exchange for this gift.

ECFA MEMBER

Glossary

Conduit gift – A nondeductible transfer of funds to a ministry that is not intended to benefit the ministry and over which the ministry does not have adequate discretion and control. Also, a transfer that has not been made to a ministry in a deductible form because the recipient ministry's function is as an agent for a particular noncharitable recipient. Also called a "pass-through" or "earmarked gift."

Contribution – See gift.

Donor-imposed restriction – See giver-imposed restriction.

Exempt purposes – The charitable, tax-exempt purposes of the ministry are generally described in the organization's governing documents.

Explicit gift restriction – An explicit gift restriction occurs when a giver sends a letter, indicates a restriction on a response form, or provides other specific communication to the ministry identifying a contribution as restricted in terms of purpose or time.

Gift – An unconditional transfer of cash or other assets to an entity.

Giver-imposed restriction – A giver's stipulation that specifies a use for the contributed asset that is more specific than the broad limits resulting from the following: (a) the nature of the organization, (b) the environment in which it operates, and (c) the purposes specified in its articles of incorporation or bylaws, or comparable documents for an unincorporated association. A restriction on an organization's use of the contributed asset may be temporary or permanent.

Implicit gift restriction – An implicit gift restriction occurs when there are certain circumstances surrounding the gift that makes the giver's restriction clear even though there is no explicit gift restriction.

Personal gifts – A transfer of money or other property from one individual to another individual, voluntarily, without any obligation nor a consideration for services rendered.

Preferenced gift – A preference indicated by a giver expressing the giver's wishes, desires, or advice (non-binding) on how or when the gift will be used but is not restricted for a specific individual. Preferenced gifts are generally recorded as restricted because the gifts are restricted for a certain purpose narrower than the organization's overall purpose.

Restricted gift – A gift that is for a purpose more specific than the broad limits imposed by the ministry's purpose and nature, such as:

1) restricted for a country,
2) restricted for a project, or
3) other time or purpose restrictions.

Short-term mission trips – A domestic or international trip sponsored by a church or other ministry for a relatively short duration, such as a week, month, or perhaps longer. Trip participants sometimes only involve adults. Other times, participants are minors, supervised by adults, or some combination of adults and minors.

Stipulation – A statement by a giver which creates a condition or restriction on the use of the transferred resources.

Endnotes

[1] I.R.C. § 170(j). IRS Publication 526 further explains that a trip participant can take a charitable contribution deduction for travel expenses only if he or she is "on duty in a genuine and substantial sense throughout the trip." A deduction will not be allowed for a trip participant with only nominal duties or no duties at all for significant parts of a trip.

[2] IRS Publication 526, Charitable Contributions, 5.

[3] Ron Shoemaker et al., "Donor Control," *Exempt Organizations Continuing Professional Education Technical Instruction Program For FY 1999*, 311–12.

[4] Letter from IRS, Exempt Organizations Division, January 2000. See also Shoemaker, "Donor Control."

ECFA's Mission

ECFA's mission is to enhance trust in Christ-centered churches and ministries.

In 1979, the founders of ECFA determined that a set of high governance, financial management, and fundraising/stewardship standards would serve the Christ-centered community well. The fundamental concept was pass/fail—ECFA's members must pass all of the standards, all of the time. Noncompliance with even one of the standards disqualified an organization from ECFA membership. Time has confirmed the wisdom of those early decisions.

In recent years, ECFA has grown at an unprecedented pace—now with over 2,000 members. We are honored and humbled by the opportunities to serve our expanding family of ECFA members. ECFA continues to increase its information and learning opportunities related to the three areas which are at the heart of ECFA's standards: governance, finances, and fundraising/stewardship. While many of these expanded avenues of learning are web-based, we provide a strong selection of webinars—with separate offerings for churches and other nonprofit organizations.

This is the day for Christ-centered organizations to step up in terms of accountability, transparency, and integrity. Accreditation by ECFA communicates credibility to givers. This enhanced giver confidence leads to greater generosity of time, treasure, and talents, which, in turn, provides increased funding to fulfill the Great Commission!

ECFA

Enhancing Trust

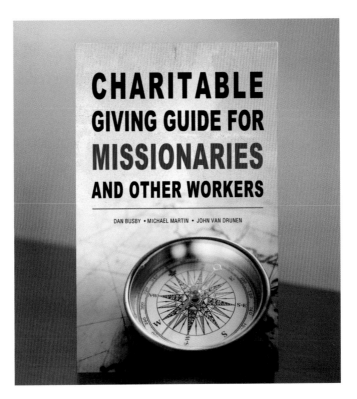

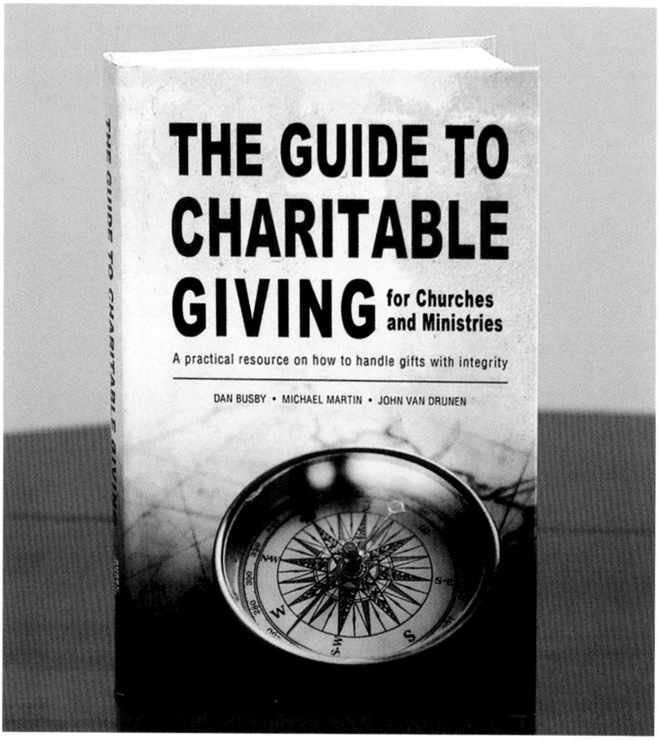
THE GUIDE TO CHARITABLE GIVING for Churches and Ministries
A practical resource on how to handle gifts with integrity
DAN BUSBY • MICHAEL MARTIN • JOHN VAN DRUNEN

Charitable Giving Guide for Giver-Restricted Gifts

by Dan Busby, Michael Martin, John Van Drunen

Properly handling gifts with giver-imposed restrictions can be challenging for many ministries. This is because these gifts present a complex combination of accounting, tax, legal, ethical, and other issues.

A giver's intentions must always be honored because the giver-ministry relationship fundamentally relies on trust.

This helpful booklet provides guidance for churches and ministries in receiving, expending, receipting, and reporting gifts restricted by givers.

Order at ECFA.org

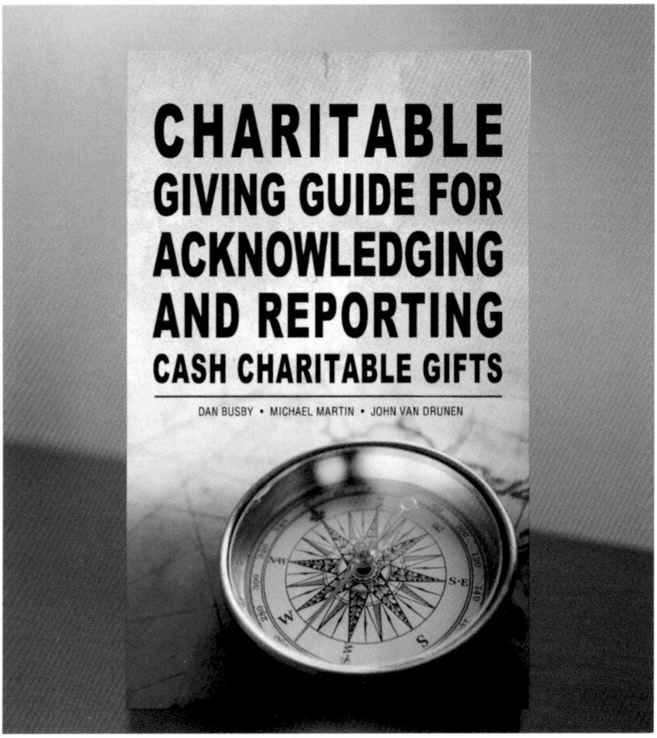

Charitable Giving Guide for Acknowledging and Reporting Cash Charitable Gifts

by Dan Busby, Michael Martin, John Van Drunen

It is a privilege for churches and ministries to express appreciation to givers for their generosity. Thanking givers for their contributions seems simple. But it is often not so. The complexity comes because U.S. tax law only allows givers charitable deductions for certain gifts, and charitable gift acknowledgments must meet strict substantiation requirements.

Providing timely and proper gift acknowledgments is an opportunity for organizations to demonstrate integrity. This requires a basic understanding of U.S. tax laws relating to charitable contributions. These rules—and more—are covered in this helpful booklet.

Order at ECFA.org

by Dan Busby, Michael Martin, John Van Drunen

Now in publication for over two decades, the *Zondervan Church and Nonprofit Tax & Financial Guide* and the *Zondervan Minister's Tax & Financial Guide* are two of the most trusted tax and financial reference guides for leaders of churches and other religious nonprofit organizations. These companion resources written by ECFA staff Dan Busby, John Van Drunen, and Michael Martin are designed to provide up-to-date information in an easy-to-understand format on key issues affecting churches and nonprofits and the ministers serving them.

Order at ECFA.org

Why Do **Churches** Join **ECFA**?

To Demonstrate **Integrity!**

Life.Church's accreditation by ECFA serves as a clear statement of assurance to our attendees, our donors, and to the public that we conduct Kingdom business with integrity and accountability.

***Craig Groeschel**, Senior Pastor, Life.Church, Edmond, OK*

Resources for Church Members

- ChurchPulse Monthly eNewsletter
- Educational Webinars and Videos
- Knowledge Center Documents
- Practical Policies for Church Use
- Church Surveys with Latest Trends
- Collaboration with Other Churches

For mor

Why Do **Ministries** Join **ECFA**?

To Demonstrate **Integrity!**

Compassion International is grateful to be a charter member of ECFA. We've found our accreditation to be immensely valuable in solidifying trust and integrity with donors throughout the evangelical community.

***Santiago "Jimmy" Mellado**, President and CEO*
Compassion International, Colorado Springs, CO

Resources for Nonprofit Members

- NonprofitPulse Monthly eNewsletter
- Educational Webinars and Videos
- Knowledge Center Documents
- Practical Policies for Nonprofit Use
- Nonprofit Surveys with Latest Trends
- Compensation Data Resource